Living with God

A family guide to the Christian faith

written by Nancy Gorrell

illustrated by Marianne Smith

~From the Author~

With love and gratitude to my parents, who first taught me to love God and to live with Him.
And with thanks to Dr Morton H. Smith of Greenville Presbyterian Theological Seminary
for his careful reading and helpful suggestions.

Christian Focus Publications

Contents

© 2000 Nancy Gorrell
Published by Christian Focus Publications Ltd, Geanies House, Fearn, Tain, Ross-shire IV20 1TW
(www.christianfocus.com ~ email:info@christianfocus.com)

Illustrations by Marianne Smith. Written by Nancy Gorrell.

ISBN 1-85792-532-7

Scripture quotations are from The New International Version,
©1973, 1978, 1984 by the International Bible Society.

This book belongs to my family.
~ Our names are ~

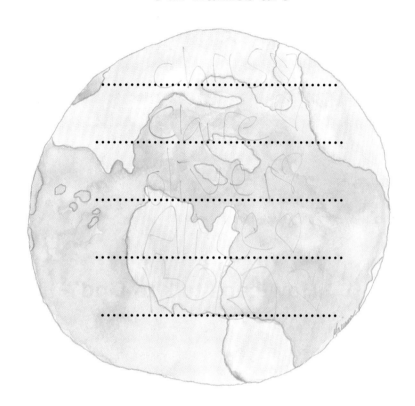

....

....

....

....

....

Look out for the memory verses at the bottom of each page.
Read and try to remember as many as you can.
Every time you learn a memory verse, you can tick a box at the end of the book.

~

As for me and my household,
we will serve the Lord.
Joshua 24:15

Worship

Heaven is the best place ever because God made it to be a perfect and excellent place of blessing for His children. It is a splendid and holy place because *God* is there. God the Father, Jesus and the Holy Spirit make heaven beautiful and bright and fill it with love and light and joy.

All the people who are there praise and bless Jesus for saving them.They love God and they love each other.

There is no place happier than heaven. There is no place more full of love.

They will be His people, and God Himself will be with them and be their God.
Revelation 21:3

There is a place that you can go to where no one ever sins. Everyone is always perfectly good all of the time. All the people there are friends. There is no fighting or crying or hurt feelings.

This place is more beautiful and amazing than you could ever imagine. Think of glorious angels, mighty heroes, pretty music and happy friends.

All these things are there and much, much more! But even these marvellous things are not the best parts about it. Do you think this place sounds like make-believe? It's not!

The Bible says that this wonderful place is called *Heaven*.

The Holy City ... shone with the glory of God, and its brilliance was like that of a very precious jewel. Revelation 21:10-11

There is a place that you can go where no one is ever sick. There are no doctor's offices or hospitals - no one there gets a runny nose or earache or an upset tummy.

There aren't even any scraped knees and there's no tangled hair!

Everyone can run and jump and dance.

Every eye can see the bright beauty; every ear can hear the sweet songs.

There will be no more death or mourning or crying or pain.
Revelation 21:4

There is a place that you can go where it will never be bedtime. You will never be tired or sleepy and there is never any night there. The sky is always bright with beautiful light. That means there is never any darkness to be afraid of and there will never be any more bad dreams!

There will be no more night.
Revelation 22:5

Does heaven seem very far away to you? You know, I have told you that this is a place where *you* can go.

How do *you* get to heaven? Do you drive in the car? Maybe you can take a bus? Can you swim there?

I know! You use a ladder, don't you?

What must I do to be saved?
Acts 16:30

"No, No!" you answer. Jesus is the one who takes you to heaven.

Jesus came to earth to live and die for His people. He obeyed for them because He knew they couldn't and He died for them so that they wouldn't be punished for their sins.

All the little children who love and trust Jesus go to heaven. God brings all of His people, whom He loves very dearly, to come to be with Him there.

"I love and trust Jesus!" you say. "I've asked Him to forgive my sins. When can I go up? It's dark here, can I go up now?"

Jesus is the One who decides when you go and you have to wait for Him to call you. Then He'll send angels to take you there. You'll be very happy, but you have to wait for Jesus.

**I desire to depart and be with Christ, which is better by far.
Philippians 1:23**

What is dying like?

Some people do go up to heaven when they are young and some people get to go when they're very little babies, but most people are old before they go to heaven. Jesus has much for them to do here first.

Then, at the right time, their bodies die and their spirits - the inside part of them, the part you can't see, the part that lasts forever - go up to be with Jesus.

The Bible calls dying "falling asleep". The outside part of you, the part you can touch, goes quietly to sleep, while your soul goes up to God. Your body rests in the ground until the day that Jesus comes back. But your soul is happy in heaven while your body is sleeping.

On the day that Jesus comes back, He will call your body up out of the ground and He will reunite it with your spirit. But your body will be better! Jesus will fix it so that it is perfect! No more stubbed toes or bruises or tummy aches.

**We believe that God will bring with Jesus
those who have fallen asleep in Him.
1 Thessalonians 4:14**

God's Bible does say that going to Heaven is a wonderful thing.

Jesus wants His people there. He loves them so much that He prays to His Father for them to come up to be with Him.

So why are people sad when the ones they love get to go there? Only because sometimes it's hard to say goodbye.

Did you ever cry when you had to leave your Granny's house? But you're very happy when you get to see her again, aren't you?

Precious in the sight of the Lord is the death of His saints.
Psalm 116:15

Just think, in heaven, you'll never have to say goodbye again!

Just one happy hello over and over again!

With the best and the happiest hello to Jesus who loved you the most!

**I will come back and take you to be with Me
that you also may be where I am.
John 14:3**

Why are people happy in heaven?

You will never be happier than you will be in heaven. You will be happy because God is there and God is the one who makes heaven perfect.

This God who makes heaven perfect loves little children just like you! You can go to heaven because He invites you to come! He sent His only Son Jesus to do everything that needed to be done so that you could go there.

And Jesus is already there now! He is praying for His people and waiting happily for them. He is very excited about welcoming His special ones to their glorious home with God!

Love Jesus. Sing songs to Him because He loved you first. Trust Him with all your heart and someday you will be able to see Jesus with your very own eyes. You will be able to look at Him, hug Him, thank Him and tell Him that you love Him.

That will be the best part about Heaven. How happy you will be!

**Father, I want those you have given me
to be with me where I am, and to see my glory.
John 17:24**

Obedience

Here are some of the little boys and girls that God made.

God created each precious one in His own image to love and worship Him.

Which one are you?

Know that the Lord is God. It is He who made us, and we are His.
Psalm 100:3

But look! These boys and girls are being naughty! They are not loving and worshipping God! Their hearts have disobedient thoughts toward God and unkind feelings toward each other.

How will these children ever be able to obey God?

There is no-one who does good, not even one.
Psalm 14:3

God knew that His little ones would have sinful hearts and would not be able to love and obey Him. So God the Father sent God the Son (Jesus) to obey for them and then to die for their sins so that they wouldn't have to be punished!

Jesus loves His people very much! He was happy to do such a hard job so that they could be forgiven.

But God demonstrates His own love for us in this:
While we were still sinners, Christ died for us.
Romans 5:8

God the Father sends God the Holy Spirit to wash His children on the inside. He cleans away all their dirty sins.

Then the Holy Spirit stays with them and lives inside them! He is the best Helper ever; He takes their hearts that still want to be bad and teaches them how to be good.

The Spirit helps us in our weakness.
Romans 8:26

God gave the Holy Spirit a special tool to use to teach His children how to obey. Do you know what it is?

It's a Book that God wrote to tell us about Himself and His world. His people love to read this book because it shows them what makes God happy and how they can live for Him.

You're right! This special Book that the Spirit uses is called the Bible.

Take the helmet of salvation and the sword of the Spirit,
which is the word of God.
Ephesians 6:17

Now that God's children have nice clean hearts, they love God and they love each other. They read their Bibles to see how God wants them to show their love. They read Jesus' words from the book of John, "If you love me, keep my commandments."

"Yes, Jesus!" they all shout. "We will obey!" But do they know what God's commandments are? Do you know? I will tell you about ten very important rules that God has given us to follow.

They are called God's ***Ten Commandments.*** God gave them to His people many years ago. They showed God's children what He was like and how to love Him and each other. You remember, of course, that God doesn't change so here are ten rules for you too!

**Whoever has my commands and obeys them,
he is the one who loves me.
John 14:21**

The first four of God's special rules tell us how we are to love God.

The first, most important thing to remember about loving God is that we are to love Him best of all! God is your Creator and your King. He has sent His Son to save you! No one will ever love you more than God and you should never love anyone or anything better than you love Him.

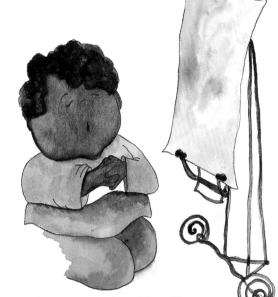

The second of God's commandments teaches us that we are to worship God and worship Him in the way that He tells us to.

Is it right for us to make a picture (or statue) of how we think God might look and then pray to the picture? No! God is a Spirit. We can't see Him so the picture we would be making would not be of God - we would be worshipping something else, wouldn't we?

Love the Lord your God with all your heart and with all your soul, and with all your mind and with all your strength.
Mark 12:30

If we love God, we will love everything about Him. We will be careful to speak reverently (worshipfully) of Him. We will love His Bible and we will love His works. God is so glorious that we will always want to learn more about Him.

The fourth of God's laws tells us to show our love to God every week on His holy day. He has called us to meet together with other Christians to worship and praise Him.

It is also good for us to rest and to grow spiritually for a whole day every week!

Praise Him for His acts of power;
praise Him for His surpassing greatness.
Psalm 150:2

What a happy day!

God's little children are home from church on Sunday and are ready to spend the week serving Him by showing love to each other.

God's next six laws teach them how to do this.

These rules remind us that God wants us to treat all people kindly. We should never do anything to anyone that we would not want them to do to us.

In everything, do to others what you would have them do to you.
Matthew 7:12

Did you know that God has given you some more very special helpers to teach you about Him and how to live for Him? You should listen carefully to what they say, love them and obey them gladly every day.

Who are these helpers?

They are your parents!

(Perhaps your home does not have a mummy and a daddy. Did you know that God has great love for you? He says so in His word. He wants you to obey and honour the ones He has given to watch over you and He wants you to trust Him. He is the protector and provider for all little children and especially for you!)

Children, obey your parents in the Lord, for this is right.
Ephesians 6:1

The next of God's commandments teaches us that life is precious.

Every person is created in God's own image and that makes him special before God.

We need to do everything we can to take care of the beautiful life that God gave us and that God gave the people around us.

Do you take care of each other by hitting or biting? Of course not! Treat one another gently and kindly.

Be kind and compassionate to one another.
Ephesians 4:32

We also learn that our homes are beautiful to God. God wants everyone to guard carefully the families that He has made.

When you are a grown-up, you must love very much the husband or wife that God gives you. Do all you can to protect the special love that you will have.

Husbands, love your wives, just as Christ loved the church.
Ephesians 5:25

God's eighth commandment says that you are not to take things that do not belong to you.

God is the one who has given other people the toys or the books or the candy that they have.

You should be glad that the Lord blesses your friends and neighbours and try to be careful with their things.

**He who has been stealing must steal no longer, but must work ...
that he may have something to share.
Ephesians 4:28**

You are also to love other people in the way that you speak to them and about them. You should never say mean words about other children and you should never, ever, say things about them that are not true.

Be kind with your mouth!
God does not want us to lie.

Do not let any unwholesome talk come out of your mouths, but only what is helpful.
Ephesians 4:29

God's tenth law tells you to be thankful for the things that God has given you.

He blesses you every day; each morning is full of new gifts from God! And remember to praise God for blessing the people around you.

Sometimes your heart wants the things that other children have.

Remember the special ways that God has shown to you that He loves you and ask Him to help you not to *covet*.

Love .. does not envy, it does not boast, it is not proud.
1 Corinthians 13:4

That is just a little about God's ten commandments! You can find them in the Bible in Exodus 20 and Deuteronomy 5.

Ask God to help you obey them every day. And every day, when you disobey, be sure to ask Him to forgive you.

Did you know that the Bible says that God's commands are not hard to keep? If you trust Jesus, God's Holy Spirit helps you to love God and the people around you and you want to obey God!

Thank you, Holy Spirit. We love you!

This is love for God: to obey His commands.
And His commands are not burdensome.
1 John 5:3

Prayer

Can someone tell me how to speak to God?

Did you know that God speaks to you every day?

Not with a big voice from heaven (saying, "Obey your mummy!") but in the strong and quiet voice of His word, the Bible.

He has many wonderful things to tell you and you will find them in His book. Little children who trust Jesus will want to hear God's words to them and they will want to talk to God too.

But how do you talk to God? Do Christian children get a telephone to heaven?

Call to me and I will answer you.
Jeremiah 33:3

God's children don't need fancy machines to talk to Him. All they have to do is pray. Do you know how to pray to the God you love?

You can pray to God in many ways.

You can talk to Him quietly, with a whisper in your heart. You can call out to Him loudly, as Elijah did on the mountain or you can sing a prayer to God, as David the shepherd boy did.

Hear my prayer, O God; listen to the words of my mouth.
Psalm 54:2

Do you have to go to a special place to talk to God? No!
You can talk to God when you're hiding under the covers
or when you are sitting in your church.

Remember, God is everywhere. He is always with you so
you can always talk to Him. The Bible says that your heart
should be ready and happy to pray to God at any time.

Pray continually.
1 Thessalonians 5:17

But what should you say when you talk to God? That's a good question and it's one that everyone, even grown-ups, need to ask. We don't always know what are the best things to ask Jesus for. We want to obey and love Him every day but sometimes we ask God for things that may not help us to do that or even for things that might hurt us!

A wonderful thing to know about God is that He even helps you to pray for what you should.

God's Spirit lives in His people and the Spirit asks for us the things that we really do need. Jesus in heaven makes our prayers beautiful and clean and brings them to His Father.

We do not know what we ought to pray for,
but the Spirit Himself intercedes for us.
Romans 8:26

One day Jesus' disciples asked Him to teach them how to pray. He was glad to do this and He taught them with a prayer simple enough for a small child to learn.

We call it the Lord's Prayer, because the Lord Jesus gave it to us.

Lord, teach us to pray.
Luke 11:1

This is what it says:

Our Father in heaven
Hallowed be your name.
Your kingdom come.
Your will be done on earth
   as it is in heaven.
Give us today our daily bread.
Forgive us our debts,
   as we also have forgiven our debtors.
And lead us not into temptation,
   but deliver us from the evil one.
For yours is the kingdom
   and the power
   and the glory
   forever.
Amen.

**So I say to you: Ask
and it will be given to you.
Luke 11:9**

This lesson from Jesus teaches us many things about prayer. We learn from it that we should always praise and bless God. We pray that the whole world will love and obey Him and will do what He commands, just as the angels do in heaven.

We also learn that God always hears us when we ask for the things we need, like our food and clothes. Isn't it wonderful that He takes care of us every day?

In everything, by prayer and petition, with thanksgiving, present your requests to God.
Philippians 4:6

In the Lord's Prayer we pray to God to forgive us for the sinful things that we do and we ask God for hearts that forgive and love others. We even ask God to keep us from being tempted to disobey Him.

Watch and pray so that you will not fall into temptation.
Mark 14:38

We worship God the King for His power and glory and for the excellent works He does in this world. We pray that He will hear us and we know that He will. God loves to listen to the little ones that Jesus has saved.

Think for a minute about what an exciting thing prayer is. At anytime and in any place, you can talk to a King - not just a rich and famous king of some country, like the king in our picture, but to the King of everything - to God who made you and who made the whole world!

**And I will do whatever you ask in my name,
so that the Son may bring glory to the Father.
John 14:13**

And think about this too - God the King wants you to pray to Him. He is happy to hear you. He's not too busy. Normal, everyday kings might think that you're too little or that you're not important enough. God doesn't think like that. He loves you.

God cares when you are sad about your broken toy or your sick granny.

He cares about whether you have food to eat or clothes to wear. He cares more than your friends, more even than your mum or your dad do.

Talk to God and tell Him when you are sad or lonely or sick and praise Him in prayer when you are happy and well.

Cast all your anxiety on Him because He cares for you.
1 Peter 5:7

God promises that He will hear you when you come to Him. Trust Him. Know and believe that God will always give you the things that will make you strong and beautiful on the inside. He will give you the things that you really need, those that will help you to love and obey Him.

You can talk to God! The King loves you. Jesus the Saviour is your friend. The Holy Spirit is your Helper.

Though you may be small to everyone around you, you are important and special to God!

Talk to this wonderful God every day and love Him with your whole heart!

**Now to Him who is able to do immeasurably more than all we ask or imagine ... be glory ... for ever and ever! Amen.
Ephesians 3:20-21**

MEMORY VERSES:

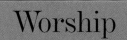

Get someone to test you to see how many verses you can remember! Tick a box when you have learnt a verse.

How great are you, O Sovereign Lord! There is no-one like you... 2 Samuel 7:22

Ascribe to the Lord the glory due to His name; worship the Lord in the splendour of His holiness. Psalm 29:2

Turn to me and be saved, all you ends of the earth; for I am God, and there is no other. Isaiah 45:22

Observe my Sabbaths and have reverence for my sanctuary. I am the Lord. Leviticus 19:30

Mary Magdalene went to the tomb and saw that the stone had been removed from the entrance. John 20:1

MEMORY VERSES:

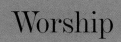

On the first day of the week we came together to break bread. Acts 20:7

Worship the Lord in the splendour of his holiness; tremble before him, all the earth. Psalm 96:9

I rejoiced with those who said to me, "Let us go to the house of the Lord." Psalm 122:1

But you have come to ... the city of the living God ... to thousands upon thousands of angels in joyful assembly. Hebrews 12:22

May the peoples praise you, O God; may all the peoples praise you. May the nations be glad and sing for joy. Psalm 67:3-4

MEMORY VERSES:

There will be no more night. Revelation 22:5

There will be no more death or mourning or crying or pain. Revelation 21:4

The Holy City ... shone with the glory of God, and its brilliance was like that of a very precious jewel. Revelation 21:10-11

They will be His people, and God Himself will be with them and be their God. Revelation 21:3

What must I do to be saved? Acts 16:30

MEMORY VERSES:

I desire to depart and be with Christ, which is better by far. Philippians 1:23

We believe that God will bring with Jesus those who have fallen asleep in Him. 1 Thessalonians 4:14

Precious in the sight of the Lord is the death of His saints. Psalm 116:15

I will come back and take you to be with Me that you also may be where I am. John 14:3

Father, I want those you have given me to be with me where I am, and to see my glory. John 17:24

The Ten Commandments

You shall have no other gods before me.

You shall not make for yourself an idol.

You shall not misuse the name of the Lord your God.

Remember the Sabbath day by keeping it holy.

Honour your father and your mother.

You shall not murder.

You shall not commit adultery.

You shall not steal.

You shall not give false testimony against your neighbour.

You shall not covet.

Exodus 20:1-17

MEMORY VERSES:

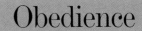

Know that the Lord is God. It is He who made us,
and we are His. Psalm 100:3

There is no-one who does good, not even one.
Psalm 14:3

But God demonstrates His own love for us in this:
While we were still sinners, Christ died for us.
Romans 5:8

The Spirit helps us in our weakness. Romans 8:26

Take the helmet of salvation and the sword of the Spirit,
which is the word of God. Ephesians 6:17

Whoever has my commands and obeys them,
he is the one who loves me. John 14:21

MEMORY VERSES:

Love the Lord your God with all your heart and with all your soul, and with all your mind and with all your strength.
Mark 12:30

Praise Him for His acts of power; praise Him for His surpassing greatness. Psalm 150:2

In everything, do to others what you would have them do to you. Matthew 7:12

Children, obey your parents in the Lord, for this is right.
Ephesians 6:1

Be kind and compassionate to one another.
Ephesians 4:32

MEMORY VERSES:

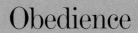

Husbands, love your wives, just as Christ loved the church.
Ephesians 5:25

He who has been stealing must steal no longer, but must work ... that he may have something to share.
Ephesians 4:28

Do not let any unwholesome talk come out of your mouths, but only what is helpful.
Ephesians 4:29

Love .. does not envy, it does not boast, it is not proud.
1 Corinthians 13:4

This is love for God: to obey His commands. And His commands are not burdensome. 1 John 5:3

MEMORY VERSES:

Call to me and I will answer you. Jeremiah 33:3

Hear my prayer, O God; listen to the words of my mouth.
Psalm 54:2

Pray continually. 1 Thessalonians 5:17

We do not know what we ought to pray for, but the Spirit
Himself intercedes for us. Romans 8:26

Lord, teach us to pray. Luke 11:1

So I say to you: Ask and it will be given to you.
Luke 11:9

MEMORY VERSES:

In everything, by prayer and petition, with thanksgiving, present your requests to God. Philippians 4:6

Watch and pray so that you will not fall into temptation. Mark 14:38

And I will do whatever you ask in my name, so that the Son may bring glory to the Father. John 14:13

Cast all your anxiety on Him because He cares for you. 1 Peter 5:7

Now to Him who is able to do immeasurably more than all we ask or imagine ... be glory ... for ever and ever! Amen. Ephesians 3:20-21

Look out for the other two books in this series

Beginning with God

God   The Bible   The Trinity

Meeting with God

Creation   Jesus   Salvation

My familys names are chris claire Oliver and Alice